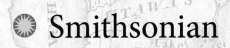
Smithsonian

Exploring
the
Virginia
Colony

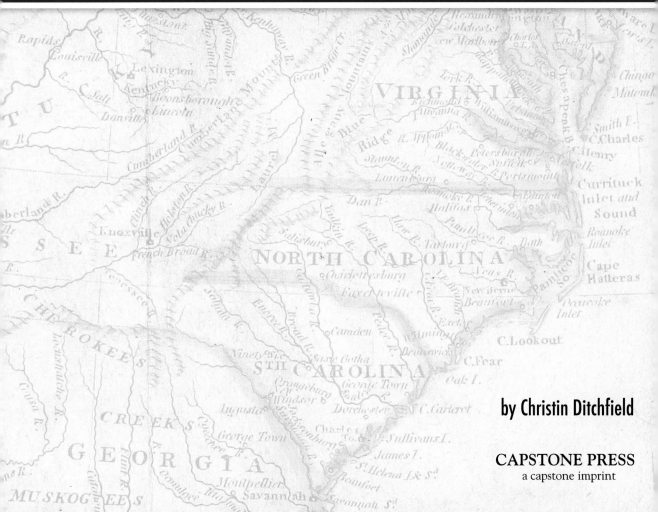

by Christin Ditchfield

CAPSTONE PRESS
a capstone imprint

Smithsonian books are published by Capstone Press,
1710 Roe Crest Drive, North Mankato, Minnesota 56003
www.capstonepub.com

Library of Congress Cataloging-in-Publication Data
Ditchfield, Christin, author.
Title: Exploring the Virginia Colony/by Christin Ditchfield.
Description: North Mankato, Minnesota: Capstone Press, [2017]
  Series: Smithsonian. Exploring the 13 Colonies | Includes bibliographical references and index.
Audience: Ages 8–11
Identifiers: LCCN 2016005496
ISBN 9781515722298 (library binding)
ISBN 9781515722427 (paperback)
ISBN 9781515722557 (ebook PDF)
Subjects: LCSH: Virginia—History—Colonial period, ca. 1600–1775—Juvenile literature.
Classification: LCC F229 .D56 2017 | DDC 975.5/02—dc23
LC record available at http://lccn.loc.gov/2016005496

Editorial Credits
Jennifer Huston, editor; Richard Parker, designer; Eric Gohl, media researcher;
Kathy McColley, production specialist

Our very special thanks to Stephen Binns at the Smithsonian Center for Learning and Digital Access for
his curatorial review. Capstone would also like to thank Kealy Gordon, Smithsonian Institution Product
Development Manager, and the following at Smithsonian Enterprises: Christopher A. Liedel, President;
Carol LeBlanc, Senior Vice President; Brigid Ferraro, Vice President; Ellen Nanney, Licensing Manager.

Photo Credits
Alamy: GL Archive, 39; Capstone: 4; Corbis: Bettmann, 33, 34, Francis G. Mayer, 35; CriaImages.com:
Jay Robert Nash Collection, 9; Dreamstime: Kclarksphotography, 11; Getty Images: Buyenlarge, 30,
Fotosearch, 37, Hulton Archive, 20, 27, Stock Montage, 7, 18, Stringer/MPI, 8, 14–15, 22, 23; Granger,
NYC: 13, 17; New York Public Library: 21; Newscom: Glasshouse Images, 10; North Wind Picture
Archives: cover, 6, 12, 24, 25, 26, 28, 31, 32, 36, 40; SuperStock: Heritage, 29; Wikimedia: Public Domain,
5, 16, 19, 38

Design Elements: Shutterstock

Printed and bound in the USA.
009669F16

Table of Contents

The 13 Colonies *4*

Virginia's Native People *10*

A New Colony *16*

Challenges and Changes
  in Virginia *22*

Slave Labor *26*

Life in Colonial Virginia *30*

The Road to Revolution
  and Statehood *36*

Timeline *42*

Glossary *44*

Critical Thinking Using
  the Common Core *45*

Read More *45*

Internet Sites *45*

Source Notes *46*

Select Bibliography *47*

Index *48*

Introduction:
The 13 Colonies

In the early 1600s, many people left Europe to make a better life for themselves. They established colonies in North America.

A colony is a place settled by people from another country. People who move to a colony are still subject to the laws of their original homeland. The new colony is like a "child" of the old country, which is the "parent" country. The parent country is in charge and makes the rules. By the early 1700s, 13 English colonies were created up and down the eastern shore of what is now the United States.

Between 1607 and 1733, England established 13 Colonies in what is now the United States.

Original Thirteen Colonies

The English weren't the first Europeans to explore North America, nor were they the first people to make their homes there. But these 13 Colonies went on to become the United States of America.

European Explorers in the Americas

In 1492 explorer Christopher Columbus left Spain in an attempt to reach eastern Asia. He thought he could get there by sailing west across the Atlantic Ocean. He didn't realize that two continents—North and South America—were in the way! After a very long ocean voyage, Columbus found himself on an island just off the coast of North America. By accident he had discovered a "New World."

After Columbus stumbled upon the Americas, explorers from Spain, England, France, Portugal, and other European countries soon followed. They brought back exciting stories of a wonderful land, rich in **natural resources**. In the late 1500s, English businessmen began making plans to **colonize** North America.

Colonial Character

Each of the American Colonies had its own unique characteristics. These differences stemmed from who settled there and why. Some were seeking religious freedom. Others wanted to find fortune and adventure. But they were all trying to create a better life for themselves in a new land. In doing so they faced many of the same challenges.

Soon after arriving in Virginia, colonists began building the Jamestown settlement.

Early English Settlement

In 1607 Virginia became the first permanent English colony in North America. That year Captain John Smith and other men built a small settlement there. They named it Jamestown after England's King James I.

Over the years Virginia became home to more and more **immigrants** from England, Wales, Scotland, Ireland, and Germany. When most of the good farmland was taken, new settlers moved further south. The southern part of Virginia later became North and South Carolina.

Captain John Smith

The Original 13 Colonies

The first permanent European settlement in each colony:

Virginia	1607	Delaware	1638
Massachusetts	1620	Pennsylvania	1643
New Hampshire	1623	North Carolina	1653
New York	1624	New Jersey	1660
Connecticut	1633	South Carolina	1670
Maryland	1634	Georgia	1733
Rhode Island	1636		

Other settlements and colonies soon followed as people from western Europe decided to make the New World their home. Some were looking to get rich. They hoped to find gold or other valuable resources that they could sell in Europe. Others simply wanted a fresh start in life. Some settlers were sent by their governments to claim the land and its resources for their home country. Many others were trying to escape their governments. They wanted to live in a place where they were free to work and worship as they pleased.

Starting a brand-new life in a strange new land wasn't easy. The settlers could bring only a few of their belongings on the long ocean voyage. Along the way they suffered hardships, hunger, and disease. But these immigrants were very brave and determined. They risked everything to create a better future for themselves and their families.

After several months at sea, the colonists arrived at Jamestown.

Critical Thinking with Primary Sources

Advertisements such as this one encouraged people to move to the Virginia Colony by describing a rich, **fertile** land that was excellent for farming. But moving to the American Colonies was risky and dangerous. The land was undeveloped, there were no towns or cities, and the native people could be unfriendly. If you were alive during Colonial times, would you have taken a chance and moved to Virginia if it could lead to a better life?

NOVA BRITANNIA.

OFFERING MOST

Excellent fruites by Planting in VIRGINIA.

Exciting all such as be well affected to further the same.

LONDON
Printed for SAMVEL MACHAM, and are to besold at his Shop in Pauls Church-yard, at the Signe of the Bul-head.
1609.

Chapter 1:
Virginia's Native People

Native Americans had been living in North America for thousands of years before the first Europeans arrived. They had their own languages and a strong sense of culture.

More than 30 tribes lived in the Virginia region alone. Most of them belonged to a group known as the Powhatan Confederacy, which was led by powerful Chief Powhatan.

The Powhatans and the Croatoans lived along the Atlantic coast. Further inland lived the Tuscaroras and Tutelo-Saponis. The Catawbas held the territory along the Catawba-Wateree River valley. The Cherokees and the Yuchis made their homes in the mountains to the west.

Chief Powhatan (c. 1545–1618)

Chief Powhatan was a ferocious fighter and a powerful leader who ruled over the Powhatan Confederacy. This group was made up of 30 tribes with a total of nearly 15,000 members. Chief Powhatan met the first English colonists when they arrived in 1607. At first his relationship with the settlers was friendly. However, conflicts and disputes soon led to war. Both sides finally agreed to live together peacefully when Powhatan's daughter, Pocahontas, married colonist John Rolfe in 1614.

Many of these tribes lived at peace with one another. Often members of one tribe married members of another. They were friends and allies. Other tribes were fierce enemies.

Daily Life Among the Tribes

Some tribes of Virginia lived in dome-shaped homes called wigwams. They wove long grass or sheets of tree bark into mats. The mats covered frames made of arched poles. This gave the homes their shape.

Other tribes built homes called longhouses that were made of trees. Longhouses looked like long, narrow barns. Several families lived in each longhouse, and several longhouses were built beside each other to form a village.

Native Americans in Colonial Virginia lived in dome-shaped wigwams.

VIRGINIA
★ USA ★

The men of the Virginia tribes hunted for deer, moose, bear, elk, turkey, and rabbit. They used bows and arrows, spears, or traps to catch and kill their **prey**. They also fished in the rivers. Tribes living near the ocean enjoyed oysters, clams, lobsters, and other shellfish.

The women took care of the home. They also grew corn, beans, pumpkins, and squash. They gathered wild rice that grew along the banks of rivers and streams. This rice was used to make many kinds of soup and stew.

Native American children also had chores to do, such as collecting nuts and berries, but they had time to play too. Girls played with dolls made from corn husks and boys played with small bows and arrows.

When the weather was warm, the Native Americans wore light clothing made of leaves, long grasses, and plant fibers. In cooler weather, men wore shirts and leggings made of animal skins. They also wore breechcloths—clothing that resembled an apron, with front and back flaps that hung from a belt at the waist. Women wore leggings or dresses. Their clothes were often beautifully decorated with shells, paint, and porcupine quills.

On special occasions, Native American men, women, and children decorated their bodies with paint. They also wore jewelry made of shells or bones and headdresses made of feathers. Both men and women had piercings and tattoos.

Native American women took their babies with them to work. In this image a baby rests on a cradleboard while Native American adults grind corn into cornmeal.

When the colonists arrived, they brought with them all kinds of things that the Native Americans had never seen before. They brought weapons, such as guns, tools, fabrics, and other household items. The tribes found that the settlers were eager to trade these items for food, land, and lumber. The settlers also wanted animal furs that they could send to Europe and sell for a lot of money.

Unfortunately the Europeans also brought diseases with them. These illnesses sometimes wiped out entire tribes. Due to disease and conflicts with European settlers, the Powhatan Confederacy was reduced to about 1,000 members by 1700.

Colonists from Jamestown enjoyed trading with local Native American tribes.

When they were at peace, the Native Americans taught the European settlers many things. They showed the newcomers how to plant and harvest a variety of fruits and vegetables that grew in North American soil. The natives also knew which plants could be used as medicines and which ones were poisonous.

Over time the Native Americans adopted some European customs. Many learned to speak English, French, or Spanish. Some also learned to read and write in these languages, which helped them create a written record of their own languages, cultures, and histories.

Chapter 2:
A New Colony

VIRGINIA
★ USA ★

In 1584 an Englishman named Sir Walter Raleigh sent a scouting party to explore the North American coast. His explorers returned with wonderful reports of a great new land that Raleigh named Virginia. They spoke of a rich land, full of natural beauty, including sandy beaches, rushing rivers, and thundering waterfalls.

The explorers also described the many different kinds of wildlife they saw in this new land. The thick forests and rolling hills were home to many species of birds, including snow geese, falcons, and bald eagles. The rivers were full of fish. The explorers thought it would be an excellent place to build a new colony for England.

Sir Walter Raleigh

In 1585 Raleigh sent seven ships carrying settlers and supplies to Roanoke Island off the coast of present-day North Carolina. The settlers began to build Fort Raleigh and a small village. However, some of these colonists made it clear that they were not interested in hard work. They wanted to search for gold. With this attitude they quickly ran out of food. When explorer Sir Francis Drake arrived in Roanoke a year later, he offered to share his food and supplies with the colonists. They asked him to take them back to England instead.

Although the first colony had failed, Raleigh did not give up. He led another group of 117 colonists to Roanoke Island in May 1587. But just like the earlier colonists, they were soon in danger of running out of food. In late August their leader, John White, sailed back to England to purchase supplies.

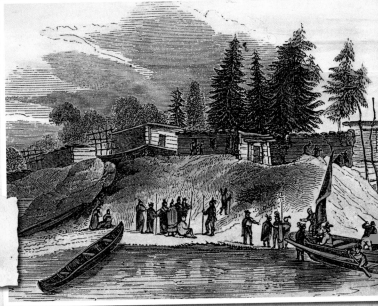

John White and a second wave of colonists arrived at Roanoke Island in 1587.

"Deer in abundance, bigger and better meat than ours in England ... Elkes of a large size ... Beasts of prey, that are profitable for their Furres, as Bevers, Otters, Foxes ... fowle of all sorts ... wild Turkies 100 in a flock, some of the Turkies weighing 40 pounds, Fish there are in great abundance of all sorts."

—a colonist describes what he saw in Virginia to his friends in England, 1649

When White arrived in England, the country was at war with Spain. As a result it was three years before White could return to Roanoke Island. When he finally did return, the colonists had disappeared. The word "CROATOAN" was carved on a fence post. Had the colonists run out of food and gone to live with the Croatoan people? Had the Croatoans attacked the fort, killing all the colonists? To this day the disappearance of the colonists at Roanoke Island is an unsolved mystery.

John White (1540–1593)

John White was an artist who traveled to Roanoke with the first English explorers in 1585. He created beautifully detailed drawings of the land, wildlife, and native people. Later White became the governor of the new colony established in Roanoke in 1587. His granddaughter, Virginia Dare, was the first child of English parents born in America.

White went back to England in 1587 to get more supplies. When he returned to Roanoke Island in 1590, all of the colonists, including his daughter and granddaughter, were missing. Unable to find them, White left the New World for Ireland, where he died in 1593.

John White and his crew tried to figure out what happened to the colonists. The word "CROATOAN" carved into a tree was the only clue left by the colonists of Roanoke Island who mysteriously disappeared.

Critical Thinking with Primary Sources

John White was an English artist and explorer. His detailed maps of the Chesapeake Bay region and drawings of Native Americans gave Europeans their first glimpse of North America. What does this drawing tell you about Native American villages?

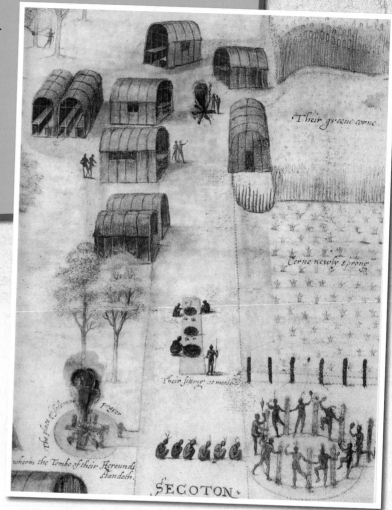

Their greene corne

Corne newly sprong

Their sitting at meate

The place of solemne prayer

wher in the Tombe of their Herounds standeth

SECOTON

Despite the failure of the settlements at Roanoke Island, a group known as the Virginia Company decided to try again. The Virginia Company was willing to pay for a group of settlers to travel to the New World. In exchange the settlers worked for the Virginia Company in the New World. They harvested crops and produced goods, such as glass. By selling these goods, the settlers could repay their sponsors from the Virginia Company. In 1606 England's King James I granted the Virginia Company a **charter** to establish a colony in the New World.

In May 1607 three ships carrying approximately 100 men and boys arrived in Virginia. Like others before them, these settlers made mistakes and faced serious hardships.

The new colonists built the Jamestown fort in a place with a good harbor for ships. Unfortunately the swampy land had little fresh water. Mosquitoes bit the settlers and spread disease. Some settlers spent all of their time building homes in the new village. Others went off hunting, exploring, or searching for gold. However, no one planted crops. So when the men got too sick or too tired to hunt or fish, they ran out of food. Within months nearly half of the colonists had died.

Soon after arriving in Jamestown in 1607, the settlers began constructing a fort.

Then Captain John Smith took over the leadership of the colony. Smith created strict new rules for the colonists. He insisted that it would no longer be every man for himself. The colonists had to work hard and work together if they were going to survive. Smith traveled to each of the Native American villages in the area trading beads and other trinkets for food. He made friends with Chief Powhatan and his daughter, Pocahontas. With Smith's help the colony grew strong again. Over time Jamestown became the first successful English settlement in the New World.

Pocahontas (1596?–1617)

Pocahontas means "playful one" in the Algonquian language. As a child the young Native American princess was very playful and friendly with the colonists. She welcomed them to the New World and taught them everything she knew about the land and its people. John Smith also claimed that Pocahontas saved his life when her father, Chief Powhatan, was going to kill him.

In 1613 Pocahontas was kidnapped by the colonists and taken to the Jamestown settlement. They wanted to exchange her for some colonists that Chief Powhatan was holding captive. Pocahontas learned to speak English and began dressing like an Englishwoman. In 1614 Pocahontas married colonist John Rolfe, became a Christian, and started going by the name Rebecca. After their marriage the colonists and the local Native Americans lived in peace with each other for several years. During a trip to England in 1617, Pocahontas died, possibly from **pneumonia**. She was only about 21 years old.

pneumonia—a serious disease that causes the lungs to become inflamed and filled with a thick fluid that makes breathing difficult

Chapter 3:
Challenges and Changes in Virginia

After a life-threatening injury, John Smith left Jamestown and returned to England in 1609. By then there were about 500 people living in the colony. Six months later only 60 of them were still alive. Soon after Smith left, the colonists started to run out of food. Without Smith they were unsuccessful at trading with the Native Americans. Instead they tried to force the natives to share their food, which made Chief Powhatan angry.

During the winter of 1609–1610, known as the "Starving Time," Powhatans attacked the colonists whenever they tried to leave the Jamestown fort to hunt for food.

Powhatan knew that the colonists were desperate for food. So instead of risking injury to his own men by attacking the colonists, Powhatan used food, or the lack of it, as a weapon. His warriors surrounded the Jamestown fort so that the settlers could not hunt for food without being attacked. The settlers were trapped inside the fort throughout the long, cold winter. This was known as the "Starving Time."

Those who survived the "Starving Time" joyfully welcome a supply ship from England in June 1610.

The hungry settlers ate whatever they could find inside the fort—rats, snakes, horses, and even the flesh of dead colonists. Many died from hunger and disease. In early June the few survivors were ready to give up and sail home to England. Just then ships arrived bringing 300 new settlers, food, and a year's worth of supplies.

On one of the ships was Thomas West, the colony's new governor. He ordered the Jamestown colonists to return to their abandoned settlement. With his help the Jamestown settlement was brought back to life.

Virginia's Cash Crop

From the moment English colonists arrived in Virginia, they struggled to survive. They had tried to make money in many ways, including selling lumber to England, but they had been unsuccessful. Finally, in 1612, John Rolfe successfully grew a type of tobacco native to the Caribbean. Rolfe's tobacco became very popular in England. He and the other colonists realized they had finally found a way to make money from all their hard work in America. Conditions in the New World were still difficult, but as news of Rolfe's success with tobacco spread, more immigrants began to settle there.

In the early 1600s tobacco became Virginia's "cash crop," which means it was grown to sell rather than feed the farmer's family.

After Chief Powhatan died, Virginia's colonists and Native Americans battled over land.

As more Europeans moved to Virginia to grow tobacco, they took more land from the Native Americans for their farms. After Chief Powhatan died in 1618, his brother took over as chief. He was not happy about the white settlers forcing his people from their land. In March 1622, after several years of peace with the colonists, the Powhatans staged a series of surprise attacks. Nearly a third of the colonists were killed. Conflicts between the Virginia colonists and the Powhatan people continued on and off for more than 20 years.

Did You Know?

In 1623 Captain William Tucker and other Virginia colonists met with the Powhatans to make peace and end the fighting. At the end of the meeting, Tucker proposed a toast, but John Potts, a doctor from Jamestown, had poisoned the Native Americans' drinks. Nearly 200 Powhatans died from the poison and another 50 were massacred.

Chapter 4:
Slave Labor

Most of the colonists who first moved to Virginia were farmers. Once the colony's tobacco industry took off, they needed help to plant and harvest their crops. At first they hired indentured servants—colonists who could not afford the ocean voyage to the New World. In exchange for help with their travel costs and living expenses, the indentured servants agreed to work for a period of time (usually seven years).

It took a lot of hard work to grow tobacco on Virginia's **plantations**. The colonists found it impossible, even with the help of servants and other paid workers. Landowners didn't want to spend all of their profits on labor costs, so they started using unpaid slaves.

Before the arrival of slaves from Africa, Native Americans were captured and forced into slavery.

"Often the husband is snatched from his wife, the children from their mother ... and no heed is given the ... prayers with which they seek to prevent a separation."

—Johann David Schoepf, a visitor to the colonies, observing a slave auction

Slavery in America

Spanish explorers were the first to capture Native Americans and force them to work as slaves. However, the natives often died from European diseases. As a result, in the early 1500s, the Spanish started bringing slaves from Africa to the New World. Many of these African slaves had been kidnapped. Others had been sold into slavery by enemy tribes. Soon many countries were making money from the slave trade.

African slaves faced a long ocean voyage under the worst conditions. Hundreds of them were chained together and forced into a very small holding area below deck. They had no space to move, no fresh air, no toilets, and very little food. Many did not survive the trip. They died of sickness, starvation, or **suffocation**. Others jumped from the ship and drowned themselves rather than face a life of slavery.

Captured Africans were crammed onto slave ships for the long journey to America.

VIRGINIA
★ USA ★

The first African slaves arrived in Virginia in 1619 aboard a Dutch slave ship. The ship's crew traded 20 slaves for food and supplies. By 1700 there were 6,000 slaves in the Virginia Colony. Fifty years later there were more 100,000, and the number only kept growing.

After they were captured, slaves were branded with hot irons. These irons burned into their flesh the name of the trading company that now owned them. They were then taken to auction houses to be sold to wealthy landowners. Once they arrived on the farms or plantations, most slaves were forced to work long hours, day after day. If they did not work hard enough or fast enough, they were beaten with whips or chains. Most of the slaves were given very little food, clothing, or shelter.

Slaves were chained to poles while they waited to be sold to wealthy landowners in America.

Not all slaves were treated so cruelly. It depended on the slave master. Some masters provided adequate food, housing, and medical care. They allowed their slaves to keep gardens and sell the produce. In this way some slaves were able to purchase their freedom. Others were set free by their masters years later.

Critical Thinking with Primary Sources

In Virginia most slaves worked on tobacco plantations like this one. What is the first thing you notice about this picture? What do you think would be the hardest thing about being a slave?

Chapter 5:
Life in Colonial Virginia

VIRGINIA
★ USA ★

With more and more people moving to Virginia in the 1700s, the colony began to grow. Towns and cities sprang up across the region. Most of the settlers were still farmers, but there were also merchants and craftsmen, such as carpenters and shoemakers. The colonists no longer had to wait for supply ships from England to bring them clothing, furniture, and other household items. They could purchase what they needed in their own colony or from another colony nearby.

Before becoming the first president of the United States, George Washington was a wealthy plantation owner. Mount Vernon, his large home, was originally built in 1735 and expanded in 1758 and 1774.

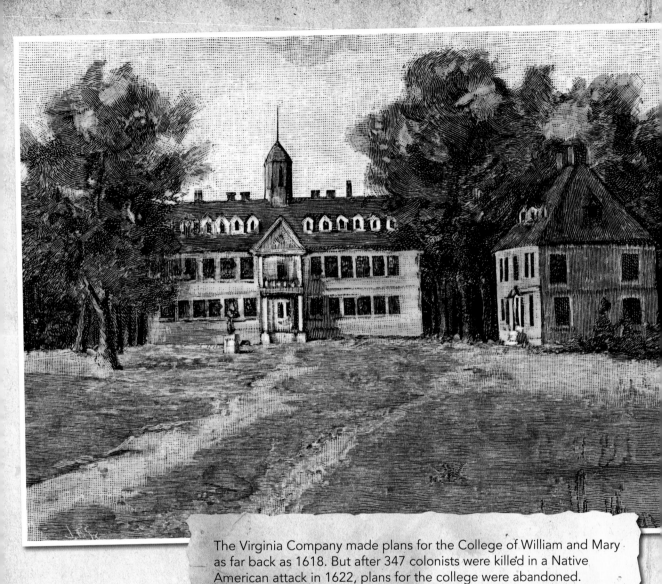

The Virginia Company made plans for the College of William and Mary as far back as 1618. But after 347 colonists were killed in a Native American attack in 1622, plans for the college were abandoned. A charter for the school was finally granted in 1693, making it the second-oldest university in the United States after Harvard.

Wealthy Virginia families still bought expensive clothing and furniture from England. They built beautiful homes on their plantations, where they held parties and dances. They had servants and slaves do the housework as well as the farming. They hired tutors to teach their young children. Older boys attended the College of William and Mary in Williamsburg or traveled to England to study.

A Day in the Life of a Virginia Colonist

In Colonial America it took a lot of hard work for most families to survive from day to day. Everyone worked together to care for the home, farm, or family business. Even very young children had chores to do.

All day long children helped their families. In towns boys studied their father's trade or the trade of another craftsman. On smaller farms boys helped their fathers with the planting and harvesting. Girls fed chickens and milked cows. They also helped their mothers with the cooking, sewing, and other household tasks. They took care of their younger brothers and sisters, gathered firewood, and carried water from the nearest river or well.

Colonial children had many chores to do around the house and farm. This girl is bringing cows to the barn to be milked.

Critical Thinking with Primary Sources

In Colonial times the phrase "playing hoops" had a completely different meaning than it does now. Now "playing hoops" refers to basketball, but hoop games date back to ancient Greece and China. Native Americans also had a similar version of the game. In Colonial times children used a hoop from a barrel and guided it with a wooden stick. They raced with their hoops and also tossed them back and forth, trying to catch them with the stick. Before modern technology, children had to create games and toys with whatever they could find. Describe a time that you made up a game or created a toy with items that you found. If you've never done so, explain how you could make a toy or game with everyday items.

During Colonial times most children did not attend school. At the time there weren't many schools. Plus the children were needed at home. Instead parents taught their children how to read and write. They had lessons in the morning after breakfast or at night after supper.

In between all the chores, Colonial children did find some time to play. They made toys out of sticks and stones and old barrel hoops that they rolled down the street. They played ring toss and bowling games, checkers, and dominoes. Boys often went hunting. Girls played with dolls made of rags, straw, or wooden spoons with faces painted on them.

After dark, families gathered around the fireplace. They took turns reading to each other from the Bible, telling stories, singing songs, or playing instruments.

Religion in the Virginia Colony

Religion was very important to people in Colonial America. Most of the colonists in Virginia were Protestants, such as Anglicans, Presbyterians, Baptists, and Quakers. At times these different religious groups were in conflict with each other. The Anglicans made up the largest group. They belonged to the Church of England—the official faith that people living in England were required to follow. Many colonists left England to get away from these strict religious rules. But some Anglicans felt that everyone living in the Virginia Colony should be required to join their church and follow its teachings.

VIRGINIA
★ USA ★

Religion was very important in Colonial America. People wore their best clothing when they attended church.

From 1734 to 1750, the 13 Colonies experienced a time of renewed spiritual growth called the "Great Awakening." Men such as Jonathan Edwards and George Whitefield were powerful preachers during this time. They inspired their followers to take their faith more seriously and live by its values. They preached that it was more important to love and serve God than to attend a certain church.

Over and over the colonists heard that all men are equal in the eyes of God. Each person is responsible for his or her own actions. People must do what they believe is right, not what is popular or comfortable or easy. These teachings may have later encouraged many colonists to fight for their freedom during the American Revolution.

During the Great Awakening, preacher George Whitefield attracted audiences with his powerful sermons.

"It was wonderful to see the change soon made in the manners of our inhabitants. From being thoughtless or indifferent about religion, it seem'd as if all the world were growing religious, so that one could not walk thro' the town in an evening without hearing psalms sung in different families of every street."

—Benjamin Franklin, on the impact of George Whitefield, whom he heard preach in Philadelphia in 1739

Chapter 6:
The Road to Revolution and Statehood

In 1754 Great Britain went to war with France in North America. Britain and France both wanted to control certain parts of North America. Some Native American tribes fought with the French, while others backed the British. The colonists fought for Great Britain, their parent country.

After winning the French and Indian War (1754–1763), Great Britain was in debt. King George III decided to tax the American Colonies to pay for the war. Hefty taxes were placed on glass, paper, tea, stamps, and other everyday items.

The colonists were furious! They believed there should be "no taxation without representation." In other words the government should not tax them unless they were allowed to participate in the government. They wanted to have a say in any decisions that affected their daily lives.

Colonists took to the streets to protest the Stamp Act.

The Colonists Fight Back

Britain passed the Stamp Act in 1765, requiring colonists to buy a stamp for printed items such as newspapers and playing cards. Many of Virginia's citizens joined a group called the Sons of Liberty to protest the Stamp Act and other unfair laws. Patrick Henry, a leading member of the group, was also a member of Virginia's House of Burgesses, the colony's lawmaking body. In May 1765 Henry delivered seven resolutions, or complaints, against the Stamp Act to the House of Burgesses. Four of them passed. One of the resolutions stated that the people of Virginia felt they should have the same rights as those living in Great Britain.

In 1766 the Stamp Act was **repealed**. But just a year later, the Townshend Acts were issued. They placed taxes on glass, paint, lead, and tea. Fed up with the king and his taxes, the colonists began **boycotting** all British goods.

The Townshend Acts were repealed in 1770, except for the tax on tea. At the time colonists consumed nearly 2 million pounds of tea per year.

Patrick Henry (far right) delivered his famous "Liberty or Death" speech less than a month before the Revolutionary War began.

"Gentlemen may cry, peace, peace— but there is no peace. The war is actually begun … I know not what course others may take; but as for me, give me liberty or give me death!"

—Patrick Henry, before the Virginia House of Burgesses, March 23, 1775

repeal—to officially cancel something, such as a law
boycott—to refuse to buy or use a product or service to protest something

The colonists began to realize that their problems with Britain could not be resolved peacefully. In the fall of 1774, representatives from 12 of the 13 Colonies met at the First Continental Congress in Philadelphia. (Georgia did not take part.) They decided that the British laws were unfair, and they began talking about forming their own independent nation. They were prepared to fight for their rights.

Back at home Virginia's leaders organized meetings and assemblies to discuss these issues. On May 15, 1776, Virginia officially declared its independence from Great Britain and created its own separate government.

VIRGINIA ★ USA ★

Thomas Jefferson (1743–1826)

As the son of a wealthy plantation owner, Thomas Jefferson grew up near present-day Charlottesville, Virginia. He began his career as a lawyer and was soon elected to the House of Burgesses. George Washington and Patrick Henry were also members.

Jefferson quickly gained a reputation as a strong supporter of America's independence. In 1775 Jefferson attended the Second Continental Congress and was asked to write America's Declaration of Independence.

Jefferson later served as governor of Virginia, secretary of state, and vice president before becoming the third president of the United States. He died on July 4, 1826, the 50th anniversary of the adoption of the Declaration of Independence.

The Colonies Go to War with Great Britain

The Revolutionary War began in Massachusetts on April 19, 1775. Most of the early battles were fought in the Northern and Middle Colonies. However, soldiers and **militiamen** from Virginia participated in these battles, including the Battles of Brandywine and Germantown in Pennsylvania.

In late 1778 the British turned their attention to the Southern Colonies, capturing Savannah, Georgia, and Charles Town, South Carolina. In 1780 British General Charles Cornwallis began moving his troops north. But Major General Nathanael Greene's **Patriot** soldiers planned to stop them. Greene tricked Cornwallis into chasing the Patriots all over the Carolinas.

In May 1781 Cornwallis began leading more than 7,000 troops across Virginia. On July 6, they met up with 4,000 Patriot troops at Green Spring Plantation near Jamestown. Leading the Patriots was France's Marquis de Lafayette, a 23-year-old general who was fighting for the Americans.

France's Marquis de Lafayette led American troops in several battles, including the one at Green Spring Plantation.

militiamen—a group of volunteer citizens who serve as soldiers in emergencies

Patriot—a person who sided with the colonies during the Revolutionary War

Although the Patriots were forced to retreat from the battlefield, Lafayette used the defeat to his advantage. The Frenchman tracked Cornwallis' movements as he led his army to Yorktown, Virginia. Lafayette wrote to Greene and George Washington asking them to meet him in Yorktown.

"This devil Cornwallis is much wiser than the other generals with whom I have dealt. He inspires me with a sincere fear, and his name has greatly troubled my sleep."

—Marquis de Lafayette, in a letter dated July 9, 1781

The British soldiers were weary and worn out. Cornwallis had lost many men and was out of supplies. By the time he and his troops made it to Yorktown, they were easily captured and forced to surrender. It was the last major battle of the Revolutionary War. The colonists had won their independence!

The British waved a white flag to signal their surrender at the Battle of Yorktown in 1781.

Jack Jouett (1754–1822)

In 1781 after the British captured Richmond, Virginia's capital city, Thomas Jefferson and several Virginia lawmakers fled to Charlottesville. While chasing General Greene and his men across the South, British General Cornwallis devised a plan to capture Jefferson and the lawmakers while they were hiding out.

On the night of June 3, 1781, Jack Jouett, a young Virginia militiaman, overheard what Cornwallis had in mind. Like Paul Revere's warning to Patriots that "the British are coming," Jouett sped off on horseback to warn Jefferson of Cornwallis' plan. After riding 40 miles across rough trails all night, Jouett arrived before dawn and warned Jefferson of the danger. Jefferson barely escaped, but the British captured seven legislators, including famous frontiersman Daniel Boone. The British let them go unharmed.

Statehood

With the war over, **delegates** from each of the former colonies met in Philadelphia to create a new government. But the representatives argued over how the new government should be organized. Smaller colonies were worried that larger colonies would be given more power and privileges.

Virginia's representatives also weren't sure they should sign the new U.S. Constitution. They were worried that it did not give some very important rights and protections to U.S. citizens. When the **Bill of Rights** was proposed, Virginia approved the Constitution. Virginia became the 10th state when it **ratified** the U.S. Constitution on June 25, 1788.

delegate—someone who represents other people at a meeting
Bill of Rights—a list of 10 amendments to the U.S. Constitution that protect important rights, such as the right to speak freely and the right to practice

Timeline

1492 Christopher Columbus arrives in North America.

1524 Italian explorer Giovanni da Verrazzano explores the Virginia coast.

1570 Spanish priests build a small settlement on the York River in present-day Virginia.

1585 The first English colony is established on Roanoke Island, but it fails within a year.

1587 A second group of colonists settles on Roanoke Island.

1590 When John White returns to Roanoke Island, all of the colonists, including his daughter and granddaughter, have mysteriously disappeared.

1607 Jamestown becomes the first permanent English settlement in North America. Virginia is the first permanent English colony in America.

1609 The "Starving Time" begins in late 1609 and lasts until June 1610 when supply ships from England arrive. Only about 60 of 500 colonists survive the Starving Time.

1612 Colonists begin growing tobacco to export to Europe.

1614 Native American Pocahontas marries colonist John Rolfe.

1617 Pocahontas dies in England.

1619 America's first elected government, the House of Burgesses, is established in Virginia. The first shipment of African slaves arrives in Jamestown.

1660 England passes the Navigation Act, requiring colonists to sell goods only to English merchants.

1734 A time of renewed spiritual growth known as the Great Awakening begins. It lasts until 1750.

1736 *The Virginia Gazette* becomes Virginia's first newspaper.

1754 The French and Indian War begins; George Washington leads Virginia's militia to fight for England.

1763 The French and Indian War ends; England defeats France and takes control of most of its North American land holdings, including present-day Canada.

1764 England taxes the 13 Colonies to pay off its debts.

1765 The Stamp Act is passed but is repealed in 1766.

1767 The Townshend Acts are passed, placing taxes on glass, paint, lead, and tea.

1770 The Townshend Acts are repealed, except for the tea tax.

1774 Virginia sends delegates to the First Continental Congress.

1775 The Revolutionary War begins in Massachusetts on April 19.

1776 The 13 Colonies formally declare their independence from Great Britain on July 4.

1777 Virginia militiamen fight in the Battle of Brandywine on September 11 and the Battle of Germantown on October 4.

1781 British General Cornwallis surrenders to George Washington on October 19 in Yorktown, Virginia.

1783 The Revolutionary War officially ends with the signing of the Treaty of Paris on September 3.

1788 Virginia becomes the 10th state when it ratifies the U.S. Constitution on June 25.

Glossary

Bill of Rights (BIL UHV RITES)—a list of 10 amendments to the U.S. Constitution that protect important rights, such as the right to speak freely and the right to practice any religion you choose

boycott (BOY-kot)—to refuse to buy or use a product or service to protest something believed to be wrong or unfair

charter (CHAR-tuhr)—an official document granting permission to set up a new colony, organization, or company

colonize (KAH-luh-nize)—to establish a new colony

delegate (DEL-uh-guht)—someone who represents other people at a meeting

fertile (FUHR-tuhl)—good for growing crops; fertile soil has many nutrients.

immigrant (IM-uh-gruhnt)—a person who moves from one country to live permanently in another

militiamen (muh-LISH-uh MEN)—a group of volunteer citizens who serve as soldiers in emergencies

natural resource (NACH-ur-uhl REE-sorss)—something in nature that people use, such as coal and trees

Patriot (PAY-tree-uht)—a person who sided with the colonies during the Revolutionary War

plantation (plan-TAY-shuhn)—a large farm where crops are grown

pneumonia (noo-MOH-nyuh)—a serious disease that causes the lungs to become inflamed and filled with a thick fluid that makes breathing difficult

prey (PRAY)—an animal hunted by another animal for food

ratify (RAT-uh-fye)—to formally approve a document

repeal (ri-PEEL)—to officially cancel something, such as a law

suffocation (suhf-uh-KAY-shun)—a lack of oxygen

Did You Know?

Virginia is known as "the birthplace of presidents" because eight presidents have been born there, including four of the first five.

Critical Thinking Using the Common Core

1. Describe what John White found when he returned to Roanoke Island in 1590 after three years away. What do you think happened to the colonists who disappeared? (Integration of Knowledge and Ideas)

2. Who was Pocahontas, and how did she help the Jamestown colonists? (Key Ideas and Details)

3. Few battles were fought in Virginia during the Revolutionary War. Name some other ways that people from Virginia contributed to America's fight for independence. (Integration of Knowledge and Ideas)

Read More

Blake, Kevin. *Roanoke Island: The Town That Vanished*. Abandoned!: Towns Without People. New York: Bearport Publishing, 2014.

Fay, Gail. *Pocahontas*. American Biographies. Chicago: Heinemann Library, 2013.

Heckt, Jackie. *The Colony of Virginia*. Spotlight on the 13 Colonies. New York: PowerKids Press, 2015.

Higgins, Melissa. *The Jamestown Colony*. Foundations of Our Nation. Minneapolis: ABDO Publishing Company, 2013.

Internet Sites

FactHound offers a safe, fun way to find Internet sites related to this book. All of the sites on FactHound have been researched by our staff.
Here's all you do:
Visit *www.facthound.com*
Type in this code: 9781515722298

Check out projects, games and lots more at
www.capstonekids.com

Source Notes

VIRGINIA
★ USA ★

Page 17, callout quote: "Carolina in 1649." *Wilmington Star-News* (Wilmington, N.C.), July 4, 1975, p. 23. Accessed March 22, 2016. https://google.com/newspapersnid=1454&dat=19750704&id=XsMsAAAAIBAJ &sjid=3QkEAAAAIBAJ&pg=3410,956322&hl=en

Page 26, callout quote: Johann David Schoepf. *Travels in the Confederation (1783–1784)*, Translated and edited by Alfred J. Morrison. Philadelphia: W. J. Campbell, 1911, p. 148.

Page 35, callout quote: Benjamin Franklin. *Autobiography of Benjamin Franklin*. Edited by Frank Woodworth Pine. New York: Henry Holt and Company, 1916, p. 192.

Page 37, callout quote: Patrick Henry. "Liberty or Death" (speech given before the Virginia House of Burgesses, Richmond, Va., March 23, 1775). Accessed March 2, 2016, http://www.patrickhenrycenter.com/Speeches. aspx#LIBERTY.

Page 40, callout quote: Marie Joseph Paul Yves Roche Gilbert du Motier, marquis de Lafayette, *Lafayette in the Age of the American Revolution: Selected Letters and Papers, 1776–1790*, Volume 4, Edited by Stanley J. Idzerda. Ithaca, N.Y.: Cornell University Press, 1981, p. 241.

Regions of the 13 Colonies

Northern Colonies	Middle Colonies	Southern Colonies
Connecticut, Massachusetts, New Hampshire, Rhode Island	Delaware, New Jersey, New York, Pennsylvania	Georgia, Maryland, North Carolina, South Carolina, Virginia
land more suitable for hunting than farming; trees cut down for lumber; trapped wild animals for their meat and fur; fished in rivers, lakes, and ocean	The "Breadbasket" colonies—rich farmland, perfect for growing wheat, corn, rye, and other grains	soil better for growing tobacco, rice, and indigo; crops grown on huge farms called plantations; landowners depended heavily on servants and slaves to work in the fields

Select Bibliography

Bell, James B., *Empire, Religion and Revolution in Early Virginia, 1607–1786*. New York: Palgrave Macmillan, 2013.

Bond, Edward L., and Joan R. Gundersen. *The Episcopal Church in Virginia, 1607–2007*. Richmond, Va.: Virginia Historical Society, 2007.

Cave, Alfred A. *Lethal Encounters: Englishmen and Indians in Colonial Virginia*. Lincoln, Neb.: University of Nebraska Press, 2013.

du Motier, Marie Joseph Paul Yves Roche Gilbert, marquis de Lafayette, *Lafayette in the Age of the American Revolution: Selected Letters and Papers, 1776–1790, Volume 4*, Edited by Stanley J. Idzerda. Ithaca, N.Y.: Cornell University Press, 1981.

Franklin, Benjamin. *Benjamin Franklin's Autobiography: An Authoritative Text*, Edited by J. A. Leo Lemay and P. M. Zall. New York: W. W. Norton & Co., 1986.

Kammen, Michael G. *Colonial New York: A History*. New York: Oxford University Press, 1996.

Schoepf , Johann David. *Travels in the Confederation (1783–1784)*. Translated and edited by Alfred J. Morrison. Philadelphia: W. J. Campbell, 1911.

Stahle, David W., Cleaveland, Malcolm K., et al. "The Lost Colony and Jamestown Droughts." *Science*, Vol. 280, April 24, 1998.

Stromberg, Joseph. "Starving Settlers in Jamestown Colony Resorted to Cannibalism." *Smithsonian Magazine*, April 30, 2013, http://www smithsonianmag.com/history/starving-settlers-in-jamestown-colony resorted-to-cannibalism-46000815/.

Index

Bill of Rights, 41
Boone, Daniel, 41

Chesapeake Bay, 19
chores, 13, 32, 33
College of William and Mary, 31
Columbus, Christopher, 5, 42
Continental Congress, 38, 43
Cornwallis, Charles, 39, 40, 41, 43

Dare, Virginia, 18
Declaration of Independence, 38
Drake, Sir Francis, 17

education, 31, 33
Edwards, Jonathan, 35

Franklin, Benjamin, 35
French and Indian War, 36, 43

games, 33
Great Awakening, 35, 43
Greene, Nathanael, 39, 40, 41

Henry, Patrick, 37, 38
House of Burgesses, 37, 38, 42

indentured servitude, 26, 42

Jamestown, 7, 20, 21, 22–23, 25,
    39, 42
Jefferson, Thomas, 38, 41
Jouett, Jack, 41

Kings of England
    George III, 36
    James I, 7, 19

Lafayette, Marquis de, 39–40

Native American tribes, 9, 10–15, 19,
    20, 21, 22, 25, 26, 27, 31
    Catawbas, 10
    Cherokees, 10
    Croatoans, 10, 18
    Powhatans, 10, 14, 25
    Tuscaroras, 10
    Tutelo-Saponis, 10
    Yuchis, 10

Pocahontas, 10, 20, 21, 42
Potts, John, 25
Powhatan, Chief, 10, 20, 21, 22–23, 25

Raleigh, Sir Walter, 16–17
religion, 34–35
religious freedom, 6, 8
Revere, Paul, 41
Revolutionary War, 39–41, 43
    Battle of Brandywine, 39, 43
    Battle of Germantown, 39, 43
    Battle of Green Spring Plantation,
        39–40
    Battle of Yorktown, 40, 43
Roanoke Island, 17–18, 19, 42
Rolfe, John, 10, 21, 24, 42

Schoepf, Johann David, 26
slavery, 26–29, 42
Smith, John, 7, 20, 21, 22
Sons of Liberty, 37
Starving Time, 22–23, 42

taxes
    Navigation Act, 42
    Stamp Act, 36, 37, 43
    Townshend Acts, 37, 43
tobacco, 24–25, 26, 29, 42
Treaty of Paris, 43
Tucker, William, 25

U.S. Constitution, 41

Verrazzano, Giovanni da, 42
Virginia Company, 19
Virginia Gazette, The, 43

Washington, George, 38, 40, 43
West, Thomas, 23
Whitefield, George, 35
White, John, 17–19, 42